MW00581223

Copyright © 2017
ISBN: 978-0-692-92434-1

"The only way you can shatter my dreams is if I give you the glass."

– Lakisha L. Tucker

This book is dedicated to all
the parents who struggle daily
to manage & maintain their
children's natural hair, while teaching
them to love and embrace who God made them to be.
To my wonderful husband who I'm thankful for, thank you for your
support, sacrifice, and love. I'm for ever grateful. To my children
Kiran, Daleeia & Ella thank you for your
unwavering support & reminding me to finish the book.
For the situation in your classroom that set the book
in the making thank-you. What the devil meant for bad,
God, meant for good. Dr. Johnny R. Freeman, frequently reminds
me that every set-back is a set-up for something greater.
This was the greater.

Tanya, this was a journey
that neither of us had traveled.
Thank you for trusting me with this vision,
and helping me to stay focused.

To the editors, Shauna Pinnix
and Felicia Freeman,
thank you for your time and
patience in editing the book.
We couldn't have done it
without you.

I just want to be me, free to walk around with my natural hair down. But what people see when they see me is not what I see.

Romans 8:28

5

I see a princess that will one day be

a **teacher**, a **queen**, a **swimmer**, or maybe all 3.

1 Peter 2:9

Should I try to make them see that...

I just want to be ME?

1 Samuel 16:7

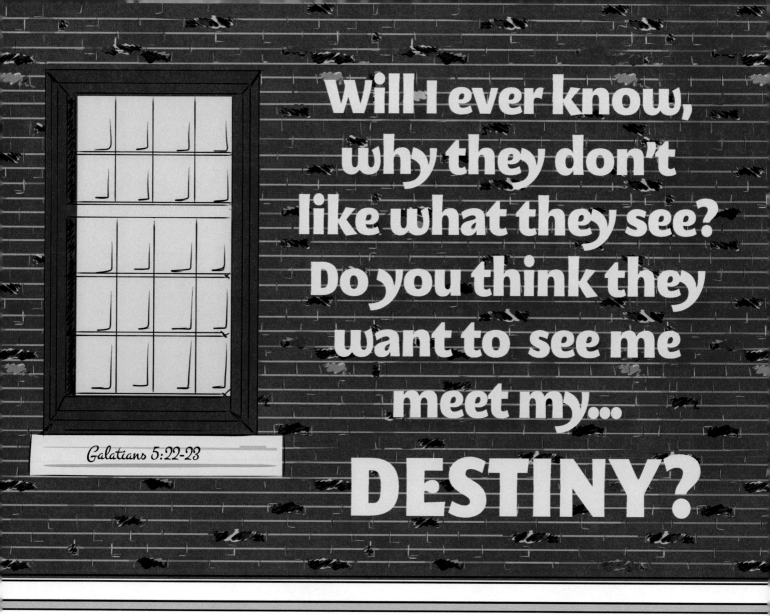

Will I ever know, why they don't like what they see? Do you think they want to see me meet my...

DESTINY?

Galatians 5:22-23

J. W. BEME
Elementary School

Perhaps they feel my hair is TOO BIG to see around...

Romans 12:2

13

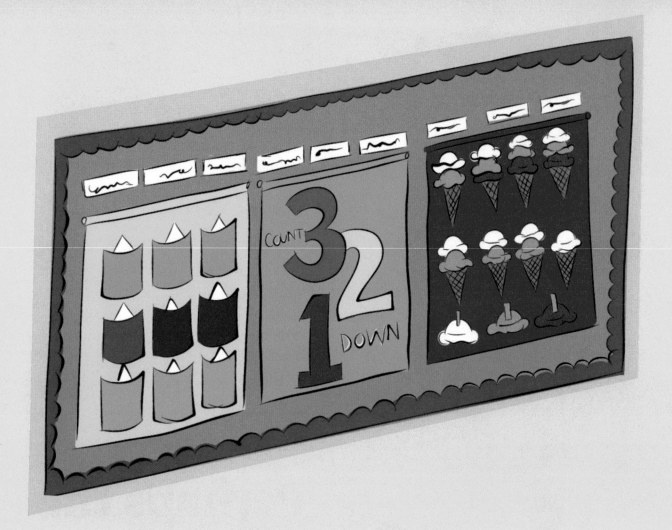

Sometimes they make me feel like a clown, you know the one with the Frown.

Genesis 1:27

But why is it that people think I should wear

my hair in this style or that?

Proverbs 24:16

Oh, I don't know, maybe they think my hair is like a flower that just grows...

Isaiah 64:8

There's a me inside of me that wants to be FREE!

Acts 17:28

What should I do?

I cannot help that I'm beautiful me.

Proverbs 24:3-4

I simply just want to be the Me I was CREATED to BE.

Ephesians 1:11

Letter to the Parents

Dear Parents,

Thank you for taking the opportunity to read Ella's story and see how she overcame. Proverbs 22:6 tells us to train up a child in the way that they should go and when they are old they will not depart from it. For Ella, she's been listening to the bible and bible stories all her life. Ella was born at 26 weeks and 1 day. So for two months and 13 days I read and sang to her. Because she was unable to drink from a bottle she was fed through a feeding tube. I'm not sure if the feeding tube had anything to do with her speech issue or not. As a parent I thought she would be picked on because of her speech, but we've never had that issue. Instead it was her hair.

I was styling her hair one morning before school and she was adamant that she couldn't wear her hair in a ponytail. I ask her why? I was informed that the teacher made a comment about the other students not being able to see around or over her hair.

As parents, we try to instill that "you are beautiful, just the way you are." There is nothing wrong with "just wanting to be you!" It was out of this situation that the book was birthed. It is my prayer that this book inspires, motivates, and allows young people the freedom of wearing their hair how they would like, and not allowing their hair to define who they are. Teach them to enjoy who God created them to be, we were all created in his image.

Parents, enjoy the pages at the end of the book. We hope this will allow you the opportunity to see your child draw and grow, or use those pages as prayer request maybe on self-image or things your young one may be struggling to overcome.

Peace and Grace,

Lakisha Tucker BA, BS, MS

Questions to the Children

1. What does it mean to be you and why do you think it is important?

2. Do you think you are beautiful? Tell why.

3. How can you encourage others who may not believe they are beautiful?

4. What do you want to be when you grow up?

5. Has anyone ever made you feel bad about yourself, if so, how did you handle it?

6. Has anyone made your friends feel sad? What did you do to make them feel better?

7. What type of music do you like to dance too?

8. Do you dance like a butterfly?

9. When you stand in the mirror what do you see?

10 Do you believe God created you too be great? Tell why.

Draw a picture of yourself dancing.

Tell why you think you are beautiful.

_____

_____

_____

_____

_____

_____

Scripture Match

Draw a line to match the book, chapter & verse on the left to the scripture on the right.

1. Romans 12:2

And we know that in all things God works for the good of those who love him, who have been called according to his purpose."

2. Acts 17:28

"Yet you, LORD, are our Father. We are the clay, you are the potter; we are all the work of your hand."

3. Galatians 5:22-23

"But you are a chosen people, a royal priesthood, a holy nation, God's special possession, that you may declare the praises of him who called you out of darkness into his wonderful light."

5. Romans 8:28

Do not conform to the pattern of this world, but be transformed by the renewing of your mind. Then you will be able to test and approve what God's will is—his good, pleasing and perfect will."

7. 1 Peter 2:9

"But the LORD said to Samuel, "Do not consider his appearance or his height, for I have rejected him. The LORD does not look at the things people look at. People look at the outward appearance, but the LORD looks at the heart."

8. Isaiah 64:8

"But the fruit of the Spirit is love, joy, peace, forbearance, kindness, goodness, faithfulness, gentleness and self-control. Against such things there is no law."

9. 1 Samuel 16:7

"In him we were also chosen, having been predestined according to the plan of him who works out everything in conformity with the purpose of his will,"

10. Ephesians 1:11

"'For in him we live and move and have our being.' As some of your own poets have said, 'We are his offspring.'"

Prayer Time

Lord, I love you because...

Lord, Thank you for...

Lord, Help me to...

53129522R00019

Made in the USA
Lexington, KY
26 September 2019